THE ARDEN SHAKESPEARE
BOOK OF QUOTATIONS
ON

The Seven
Ages of Man

Compiled by
JANE ARMSTRONG

AS

The Arden website is at
http://www.ardenshakespeare.com

First published 2001 by The Arden Shakespeare

This Collection Copyright © 2001 Jane Armstrong

Arden Shakespeare is an imprint of Thomson Learning

Thomson Learning
Berkshire House
168–173 High Holborn
London WC1V 7AA

Designed and typeset by Martin Bristow

Printed in Singapore by Seng Lee Press

British Library Cataloguing in Publication Data
A catalogue record for this book is available from the British Library

Library of Congress Cataloguing in Publication Data
A catalogue record has been requested

ISBN 1-903436-52-4

NPN 9 8 7 6 5 4 3 2 1

The Seven
Ages of Man

THE ARDEN SHAKESPEARE
BOOKS OF QUOTATIONS

Life

Love

Death

Nature

Songs & Sonnets

The Seven Ages of Man

All the world's a stage,
And all the men and women merely players.
They have their exits and their entrances,
And one man in his time plays many parts,
His acts being seven ages. At first the infant,
Mewling and puking in the nurse's arms.
Then, the whining school-boy with his satchel
And shining morning face, creeping like snail
Unwillingly to school. And then the lover,
Sighing like furnace, with a woeful ballad
Made to his mistress' eyebrow. Then, a soldier,
Full of strange oaths, and bearded like the pard,
Jealous in honour, sudden, and quick in quarrel,
Seeking the bubble reputation
Even in the cannon's mouth. And then, the justice,
In fair round belly, with good capon lined,
With eyes severe, and beard of formal cut,
Full of wise saws, and modern instances,
And so he plays his part. The sixth age shifts
Into the lean and slippered pantaloon,
With spectacles on nose, and pouch on side,
His youthful hose well saved, a world too wide
For his shrunk shank, and his big manly voice,

Turning again toward childish treble, pipes
And whistles in his sound. Last scene of all,
That ends this strange eventful history,
Is second childishness and mere oblivion,
Sans teeth, sans eyes, sans taste, sans everything.

As You Like It 2.7.139–66

1
Infancy

Truth shall nurse her,
Holy and heavenly thoughts still counsel her.

Henry VIII 5.4.28–9

Wife and child
Those precious motives, those strong knots of love.

Macbeth 4.3.26–7

Our joy,
Although our last and least.

King Lear 1.1.82–3

Thou met'st with things dying,
I with things new-born.

Winter's Tale 3.3.111–12

Almost at fainting under
The pleasing punishment that women bear.

Comedy of Errors 1.1.45–6

When we are born we cry that we are come
To this great stage of fools.

King Lear 4.6.178–9

Poor inch of nature!

Pericles 3.1.34

She came in great with child; and longing,
saving your honours' reverence, for stewed prunes.

Measure for Measure 2.1.87–8

We came crying hither:
Thou knowst that the first time we smell the air
We wawl and cry.

King Lear 4.6.174–6

I have given suck, and know
How tender 'tis to love the babe that milks me.

Macbeth 1.7.54–5

A grievous burden was thy birth to me;
Tetchy and wayward was thy infancy.

Richard III 4.4.168–9

A devil, a born devil, on whose nature
Nurture can never stick.

Tempest 4.1.188–9

Nature makes them partial.

Hamlet 3.3.32 – on mothers

Die single, and thine image dies with thee.

Sonnet 3

2
Childhood

Two lads that thought there was no more behind,
But such a day tomorrow as today,
And to be boy eternal.

Winter's Tale 1.2.63–5

Those that do teach young babes
Do it with gentle means and easy tasks.

Othello 4.2.113–14

Thou art thy mother's glass, and she in thee
Calls back the lovely April of her prime.

Sonnet 3

In maiden meditation, fancy-free.

Midsummer Night's Dream 2.1.164

Is all forgot?
All school-days' friendship, childhood innocence?
We, Hermia, like two artificial gods,
Have with our needles created both one flower,
Both on one sampler, sitting on one cushion,
Both warbling of one song, both in one key,
As if our hands, our sides, voices and minds,
Had been incorporate. So we grew together,
Like to a double cherry, seeming parted,
But yet an union in partition,
Two lovely berries moulded on one stem.

Midsummer Night's Dream 3.2.201–11

She was a vixen when she went to school.

Midsummer Night's Dream 3.2.324

He makes a July's day as short as December.

Winter's Tale 1.2.169

No, trust me, she is peevish, sullen, froward,
Proud, disobedient, stubborn, lacking duty,
Neither regarding that she is my child,
Nor fearing me as if I were her father.

Two Gentlemen of Verona 3.1.68–71

'Tis not good that children should know any wickedness.

Merry Wives of Windsor 2.2.120–1

Pitchers have ears.

Richard III 2.4.37

Grief fills the room up of my absent child,
Lies in his bed, walks up and down with me,
Puts on his pretty looks, repeats his words,
Remembers me of all his gracious parts,
Stuffs out his vacant garments with his form;
Then have I reason to be fond of grief?
Fare you well: had you such a loss as I
I could give better comfort than you do . . .
O Lord! my boy, my Arthur, my fair son!
My life, my joy, my food, my all the world!
My widow-comfort, and my sorrow's cure!

King John 3.3.93–100, 103–5

I have done nothing but in care of thee,
Of thee, my dear one, thee my daughter.

Tempest 1.2.16–17

3
Youth

My salad days,
When I was green in judgement.

Antony and Cleopatra 1.5.76–7

Crabbed age and youth cannot live together:
Youth is full of pleasance, age is full of care;
Youth like summer morn, age like winter weather;
Youth like summer brave, age like winter bare.
Youth is full of sport, age's breath is short;
　　Youth is nimble, age is lame;
Youth is hot and bold, age is weak and cold;
　　Youth is wild and age is tame.
Age, I do abhor thee; youth, I do adore thee:
　　O my love, my love is young!
Age, I do defy thee. O sweet shepherd, hie thee,
　　For methinks thou stays too long.

Passionate Pilgrim 12

He wears the rose
Of youth upon him.

Antony and Cleopatra 3.13.20–1

As full of spirit as the month of May,
And gorgeous as the sun at midsummer.

1 Henry IV 4.1.101–2

How green you are and fresh in this old world!

King John 3.3.145

In the very May-morn of his youth,
Ripe for exploits and mighty enterprises.

Henry V 1.2.120–1

Young, and so unkind!

Venus and Adonis 187

Briefly die their joys
That place them on the truth of girls and boys.

Cymbeline 5.5.106–7

LEAR So young and so untender?
CORDELIA So young, my lord, and true.

King Lear 1.1.107–8

You speak like a green girl.

Hamlet 1.3.101

Not yet old enough for a man, nor young enough for a boy: as a squash is before 'tis a peascod, or a codling when 'tis almost an apple. 'Tis with him in standing water, between boy and man.

Twelfth Night 1.5.153–6

He capers, he dances, he has eyes of youth, he writes verses, he speaks holiday, he smells April and May.

Merry Wives of Windsor 3.2.60–2

What! A young knave, and begging! Is there not wars? Is there not employment? Doth not the King lack subjects? Do not the rebels need soldiers?

2 Henry IV 1.2.72–4

Youth to itself rebels, though none else near.

Hamlet 1.3.44

Though the camomile, the more it is trodden on the faster it grows, yet youth, the more it is wasted the sooner it wears.

1 Henry IV 2.4.396–8

Oft expectation fails, and most oft there
Where most it promises.

All's Well That Ends Well 2.1.141–2

I never knew so young a body with so old a head.

Merchant of Venice 4.1.161–2

Would there were no age between ten and three-and-twenty, or that youth would sleep out the rest; for there is nothing in the between but getting wenches with child, wronging the ancientry, stealing, fighting.

Winter's Tale 3.3.59–63

A man can no more separate age and covetousness than a can part young limbs and lechery.

2 Henry IV 1.2.228–30

Why should a man whose blood is warm within, Sit like his grandsire, cut in alabaster?

Merchant of Venice 1.1.83–4

YOUNG LOVE

In delay there lies no plenty,
Then come kiss me, sweet and twenty:
    Youth's a stuff will not endure.

Twelfth Night 2.3.50–2

Lovers and madmen have such seething brains,
Such shaping fantasies, that apprehend
More than cool reason ever comprehends.
The lunatic, the lover, and the poet
Are of imagination all compact.

Midsummer Night's Dream 5.1.4–8

Time goes on crutches till love hath all his rites.

Much Ado About Nothing 2.1.336–7

In the holiday-time of my beauty.

Merry Wives of Windsor 2.1.1–2

See, where she comes apparelled like the spring.

Pericles 1.1.13

Beauty is a witch.
Against whose charms faith melteth into blood.

Much Ado About Nothing 2.1.170–1

Where is any author in the world
Teaches such beauty as a woman's eye?

Love's Labour's Lost 4.3.308–9

Young men's love then lies
Not truly in their hearts but in their eyes.

Romeo and Juliet 2.3.63–4

A dangerous and lascivious boy, who is a whale
to virginity, and devours up all the fry it finds.

All's Well That Ends Well 4.3.216–17

For Hamlet, and the trifling of his favour,
Hold it a fashion and a toy in blood,
A violet in the youth of primy nature,
Forward, not permanent, sweet, not lasting,
The perfume and suppliance of a minute,
No more.

Hamlet 1.3.5–10

4
Maturity

Things won are done; joy's soul lies in the doing.

Troilus and Cressida 1.2.280

What piece of work is a man, how noble in reason,
how infinite in faculties, in form and moving how
express and admirable, in action how like an angel,
in apprehension how like a god: the beauty of the world,
the paragon of animals.

Hamlet 2.2.305–9

A breathing valiant man
Of an invincible unconquered spirit.

1 Henry VI 4.2.31–2

To business that we love we rise betime
And go to't with delight.

Antony and Cleopatra 4.4.20–1

His years but young, but his experience old.

Two Gentlemen of Verona 2.4.68

The younger rises when the old doth fall.

King Lear 3.3.25

He doth bestride the narrow world
Like a Colossus.

Julius Caesar 1.2.134–5

I have trod a measure, I have flattered a lady,
I have been politic with my friend, smooth with mine
enemy, I have undone three tailors, I have had four
quarrels, and like to have fought one.

As You Like It 5.4.43–6

You come in faint for want of meat, depart reeling
with too much drink: sorry that you have paid
too much, and sorry that you are paid too much:
purse and brain, both empty.

Cymbeline 5.4.160–3

Company, villainous company, hath been the spoil of me.

1 Henry IV 3.3.9–10

Who would be a father?

Othello 1.1.162

How sharper than a serpent's tooth it is
To have a thankless child.

King Lear 1.4.280–1

For this the foolish over-careful fathers
Have broke their sleep with thoughts,
Their brains with care, their bones with industry.

2 Henry IV 4.5.67–9

5
Middle Age

Not so young to love a woman for singing,
nor so old to dote on her for anything.
I have years on my back forty-eight.

King Lear 1.4.37–9

Our loves and comforts should increase
Even as our days do grow.

Othello 2.1.192–3

Tomorrow, and tomorrow, and tomorrow,
Creeps in this petty pace from day to day.

Macbeth 5.5.19–20

How use doth breed a habit in a man!

Two Gentlemen of Verona 5.4.1

When forty winters shall besiege thy brow,
And dig deep trenches in thy beauty's field,
Thy youth's proud livery, so gazed on now,
Will be a tattered weed of small worth held.

Sonnet 2

    At your age
The heyday in the blood is tame, it's humble,
And waits upon the judgement.

Hamlet 3.4.68–70

Though we are justices and doctors and churchmen,
Master Page, we have some salt of our youth in us.

Merry Wives of Windsor 2.3.42–4

To me, fair friend, you never can be old;
For as you were when first your eye I eyed,
Such seems your beauty still: three winters cold
Have from the forests shook three summers' pride;
Three beauteous springs to yellow autumn turned
In process of the seasons have I seen;
Three April perfumes in three hot Junes burned,
Since first I saw you fresh, which yet art green.
Ah, yet doth beauty, like a dial hand,
Steal from his figure, and no pace perceived;
So your sweet hue, which methinks still doth stand,
Hath motion, and mine eye may be deceived;
  For fear of which, hear this, thou age unbred,
  Ere you were born was beauty's summer dead.

Sonnet 104

Think on me
That am with Phoebus' amorous pinches black
And wrinkled deep in time . . .
When thou wast here above the ground, I was
A morsel for a monarch.

Antony and Cleopatra 1.5.28–32

Age cannot wither her, nor custom stale
Her infinite variety.

Antony and Cleopatra 2.2.245–6

With mirth and laughter let old wrinkles come.

Merchant of Venice 1.1.80

KENT You have that in your countenance which I
   would fain call master.
LEAR What's that?
KENT Authority.

King Lear 1.4.27–30

Experience is by industry achieved,
And perfected by the swift course of time.

Two Gentlemen of Verona 1.3.22–3

Lowliness is young ambition's ladder
Whereto the climber upward turns his face;
But when he once attains the upmost round
He then unto the ladder turns his back,
Looks in the clouds, scorning the base degrees
By which he did ascend.

Julius Caesar 2.1.22–7

6
Declining Years

When I do count the clock that tells the time,
And see the brave day sunk in hideous night;
When I behold the violet past prime,
And sable curls all silvered o'er with white:
When lofty trees I see barren of leaves,
Which erst from heat did canopy the herd,
And summer's green all girded up in sheaves
Borne on the bier with white and bristly beard:
Then of thy beauty do I question make,
That thou among the wastes of time must go,
Since sweets and beauties do themselves forsake,
And die as fast as they see others grow,
    And nothing 'gainst time's scythe can make defence
    Save breed to brave him, when he takes thee hence.

Sonnet 12

When to the sessions of sweet silent thought
I summon up remembrance of things past.

Sonnet 30

You and I are past our dancing days.

Romeo and Juliet 1.5.32

We have seen better days.

As You Like It 2.7.120

Jesu, Jesu, the mad days that I have spent! And to see
how many of my old acquaintance are dead!

2 Henry IV 3.2.33–5

That trunk of humours, that bolting-hutch of beastliness, that swollen parcel of dropsies, that huge bombard of sack, that stuffed cloak-bag of guts, that roasted Manningtree ox with the pudding in his belly, that reverend vice, that grey iniquity, that father ruffian, that vanity in years.

1 Henry IV 2.4.443–8

If to be old and merry be a sin, then many an old host that I know is damned.

1 Henry IV 2.4.465–6

Is it not strange that desire should so many years outlive performance?

2 Henry IV 2.4.260–1

We have heard the chimes at midnight, Master Shallow.

2 Henry IV 3.2.214–15

What doth gravity out of his bed at midnight?

1 Henry IV 2.4.290–1

Have you not a moist eye, a dry hand, a yellow cheek,
a white beard, a decreasing leg, an increasing belly?
Is not your voice broken, your wind short, your chin
double, your wit single, and every part about you
blasted with antiquity?

2 Henry IV 1.2.180–4

How ill white hairs becomes a fool and jester!

2 Henry IV 5.5.48

Old folks . . .
Unwieldy, slow, heavy, and pale as lead.

Romeo and Juliet 2.5.16–17

And then, sir, does a this – a does – what was I about
to say? By the mass, I was about to say something.
Where did I leave?

Hamlet 2.1.50–3

These tedious old fools.

Hamlet 2.2.219

A good old man, sir, he will be talking; as they say,
'When the age is in, the wit is out.'

Much Ado About Nothing 3.5.32–3

Why art thou old and yet not wise?

Lucrece 1550

For we are old, and on our quick'st decrees
Th'inaudible and noiseless foot of time
Steals ere we can effect them.

All's Well That Ends Well 5.3.40–2

I feel
The best is past.

Tempest 3.3.50–1

You shall mark
Many a duteous and knee-crooking knave
That, doting on his own obsequious bondage,
Wears out his time much like his master's ass
For nought but provender, and when he's old, cashiered.

Othello 1.1.43–7

His silver hairs
Will purchase us a good opinion.

Julius Caesar 2.1.143–4

Give me a staff of honour for mine age,
But not a sceptre to control the world.

Titus Andronicus 1.1.201–2

Eternal love . . .
Weighs not the dust and injury of age.

Sonnet 108

That which should accompany old age,
As honour, love, obedience, troops of friends.

Macbeth 5.3.24–5

All's well that ends well; still the fine's the crown.
Whate'er the course, the end is the renown.

All's Well That Ends Well 4.4.35–6

7
Old Age

That time of year thou mayst in me behold,
When yellow leaves, or none, or few do hang
Upon those boughs which shake against the cold,
Bare ruined choirs where late the sweet birds sang;
In me thou seest the twilight of such day
As after sunset fadeth in the west,
Which by and by black night doth take away,
Death's second self that seals up all in rest;
In me thou seest the glowing of such fire
That on the ashes of his youth doth lie,
As the deathbed, whereon it must expire,
Consumed with that which it was nourished by;
  This thou perceiv'st, which makes thy love more strong,
  To love that well, which thou must leave ere long.

Sonnet 73

Old men forget.

Henry V 4.3.49

Unregarded age in corners thrown.

As You Like It 2.3.42

You are old:
Nature in you stands on the very verge
Of her confine. You should be ruled and led
By some discretion that discerns your state
Better than you yourself.

King Lear 2.2.338–42

He that doth the ravens feed,
Yea providently caters for the sparrow,
Be comfort to my age.

As You Like It 2.3.43–5

My age is as a lusty winter,
Frosty, but kindly.

As You Like It 2.3.52–3

My old bones aches.

Tempest 3.3.2

I am too old to learn.

King Lear 2.2.128

'Tis the infirmity of his age, yet he hath ever but slenderly known himself.

King Lear 1.1.294–5

Pray you now, forget and forgive; I am old and foolish.

King Lear 4.7.83–4

A poor, infirm, weak and despised old man.

King Lear 3.2.20

O ruined piece of nature, this great world
Shall so wear out to naught.

King Lear 4.6.130–1

Pray do not mock me.
I am a very foolish, fond old man,
Fourscore and upward, not an hour more nor less;
And to deal plainly,
I fear I am not in my perfect mind.

King Lear 4.7.59–63

Sir, I am vexed;
Bear with my weakness; my old brain is troubled.
Be not disturbed with my infirmity.

Tempest 4.1.158–60

O, if this were seen,
The happiest youth, viewing his progress through,
What perils past, what crosses to ensue,
Would shut the book and sit him down and die.

2 Henry IV 3.1.53–6

I have lived long enough: my way of life
Is fall'n into the sere, the yellow leaf.

Macbeth 5.3.22–3

I have a journey, sir, shortly to go;
My master calls me, I must not say no.

King Lear 5.3.320–1

More are men's ends marked than their lives before.
The setting sun, and music at the close,
As the last taste of sweets, is sweetest last,
Writ in remembrance more than things long past.

Richard II 2.1.11–14

Men must endure
Their going hence even as their coming hither.
Ripeness is all.

King Lear 5.2.9–11

Fear no more the heat o'th' sun,
    Nor the furious winter's rages,
Thou thy worldly task has done,
    Home art gone and ta'en thy wages.
Golden lads and girls all must,
As chimney-sweepers, come to dust. . . .
The sceptre, learning, physic, must
All follow this and come to dust.

Cymbeline 4.2.258–63, 68–9

I am old, I am old.

2 Henry IV 2.4.271

[47]

Like as the waves make towards the pebbled shore,
So do our minutes hasten to their end,
Each changing place with that which goes before,
In sequent toil all forwards do contend.
Nativity, once in the main of light,
Crawls to maturity; wherewith being crowned
Crooked eclipses 'gainst his glory fight,
And time, that gave, doth now his gift confound.
Time doth transfix the flourish set on youth
And delves the parallels in beauty's brow;
Feeds on the rarities of nature's truth,
And nothing stands but for his scythe to mow.
  And yet to times in hope my verse shall stand,
  Praising thy worth, despite his cruel hand.

Sonnet 60